D0982391

AMAZING ORIGAMI

Snapping and Speaking Origami

Joe Fullman

Woof!

Gareth Stevens
PUBLISHING

SOMERSET CO. LIBRARY
BRIDGEWATER, N.J. 08807

Please visit our website, www.garethstevens.com. For a free color catalog of all our high-quality books, call toll free 1-800-542-2595 or fax 1-877-542-2596.

Cataloging-in-Publication Data
Fullman, Joe.
Snapping and speaking origami / by Joe Fullman.
p. cm. — (Amazing origami)
Includes index.
ISBN 978-1-4824-4175-8 (pbk.)
ISBN 978-1-4824-4176-5 (6-pack)
ISBN 978-1-4824-4177-2 (library binding)
1. Origami — Juvenile literature. I. Fullman, Joe. II. Title.
TT870.F85 2016
736'.982—d23

First Edition

Published in 2016 by
Gareth Stevens Publishing
111 East 14th Street, Suite 349
New York, NY 10003

Copyright © 2016 Arcturus Publishing

Models and photography: Belinda Webster and Michael Wiles
Text: Joe Fullman
Design: Emma Randall
Editor: Frances Evans

All rights reserved. No part of this book may be reproduced in any form without permission in writing from the publisher, except by a reviewer.

Printed in the United States of America
CPSIA compliance information: Batch CW16GS: For further information contact Gareth Stevens, New York, New York at 1-800-542-2595.

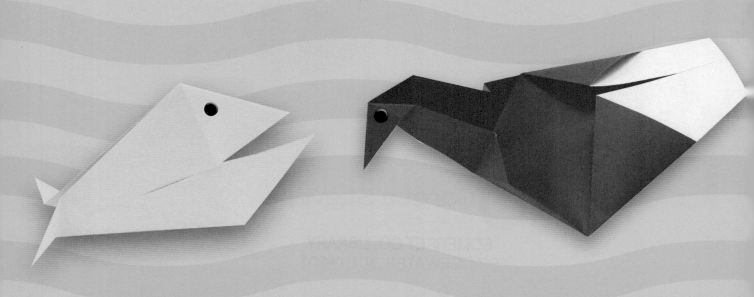

Contents

Basic Folds

Origami has been popular in Japan for hundreds of years and is now loved all around the world. You can make great models with just one sheet of paper... and this book shows you how!

The paper used in origami is thin but strong, so that it can be folded many times. It is usually colored on one side. Alternatively you can use ordinary scrap paper, but make sure it's not too thick.

Origami models often share the same folds and basic designs. This introduction explains some of the folds that you will need for the projects in this book, and they will also come in useful if you make other origami models. When making the models in this book, follow the key below to find out what the lines and arrows mean. And always crease well!

KEY

valley fold – – – – – – – –

mountain fold ....

step fold (mountain and valley fold next to each other)

direction to move paper

push ◄

MOUNTAIN FOLD

To make a mountain fold, fold the paper so that the crease is pointing up towards you, like a mountain.

VALLEY FOLD

To make a valley fold, fold the paper the other way, so that the crease is pointing away from you, like a valley.

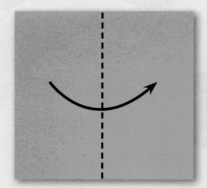

A NOTE ABOUT MEASUREMENTS

Measurements are given in U.S. form with the metric in parentheses. The metric conversion is rounded to make it easier to measure.

INSIDE REVERSE FOLD

An inside reverse fold is useful if you want to make a nose or a tail, or if you want to flatten off the shape of another part of an origami model.

Open

1 Practice by first folding a piece of paper diagonally in half. Make a valley fold on one point and crease.

2 It's important to make sure that the paper is creased well. Run your finger over the crease two or three times.

3 Unfold and open up the corner slightly. Refold the crease nearest to you into a mountain fold.

4 Open up the paper a little more and then tuck the tip of the point inside. Close the paper. This is the view from the underside of the paper.

5 Flatten the paper. You now have an inside reverse fold.

OUTSIDE REVERSE FOLD

An outside reverse fold is useful if you want to make a head, beak or foot, or another part of your model that sticks out.

open

1 Practice by first folding a piece of paper diagonally in half. Make a valley fold on one point and crease.

2 It's important to make sure that the paper is creased well. Run your finger over the crease two or three times.

3 Unfold and open up the corner slightly. Refold the crease furthest away from you into a valley fold.

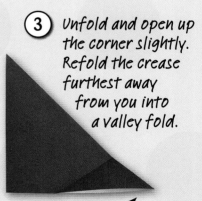

4 Open up the paper a little more and start to turn the corner inside out. Then close the paper when the fold begins to turn.

5 You now have an outside reverse fold. You can either flatten the paper or leave it rounded out.

Gulping Fish

It only takes a few minutes of careful paper folding to create this hungry origami fish with its great, gulping mouth.

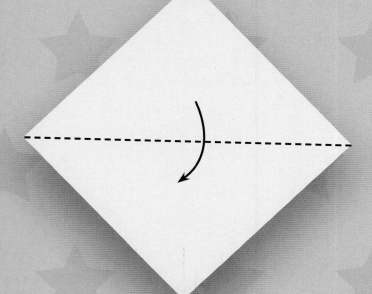

1. Place your paper white side up, with a corner facing you. Valley fold it in half from top to bottom, then unfold.

2. Valley fold the bottom corner up to the center line.

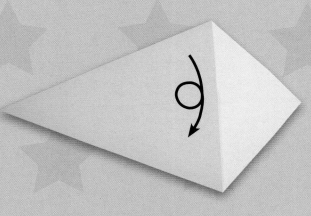

3. Valley fold the top corner down to the center line.

4. Your paper should look like this. Turn it over from top to bottom.

8

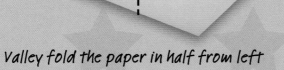

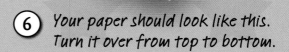

(5) Valley fold the paper in half from left to right.

(6) Your paper should look like this. Turn it over from top to bottom.

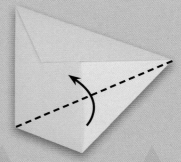

(7) Fold the top corner down to the center line.

(8) Fold the bottom corner up to the center line.

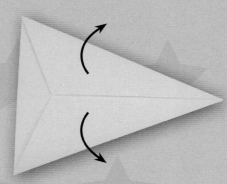

Open

(9) Your paper should look like this. Unfold the folds you made in steps 7 and 8, but leave the corners sticking up in the air.

(10) Open up the horizontal flap in the center and push it to the left.

Did You Know?

The biggest fish mouth on Earth belongs to the whale shark. A really big shark can grow up to 62 feet (19 m) long and has a mouth 5 feet (1.5 m) wide.

Push

11 As you push, the top and bottom flaps will start to fold inwards, forming this shape. Flatten the paper down.

12 On the top layer, fold up the right point, as shown. This will be the first tail fin.

13 Your paper should look like this. Turn it over from top to bottom.

14 Make another fold on the right-hand side, as shown, to form the second tail fin.

15 Your snapping origami fish is ready.

Pull

Pull

16 To make your fish gulp, simply take a tail fin in each hand. When you pull them apart, your fish will open his mouth. And when you push them together, he'll snap it shut again!

Pecking Chicken

Peck, peck, peck! Follow these instructions to make a paper chicken that pecks at the ground, just like a real bird hunting for tasty things to eat.

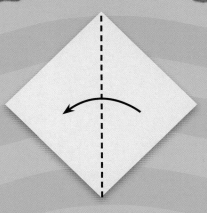

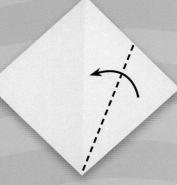

1. Place the paper white side up, with a corner facing you. Valley fold it in half from right to left, then unfold.

2. Valley fold the right-hand point to the center.

3. Valley fold the left-hand point to the center.

4. Your paper should look like this. Turn it over from left to right.

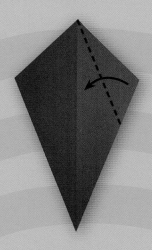

5. Fold the right point to the center line.

6. Fold the left point to the center line.

⑦ Flip the paper over from left to right, and then rotate it 90° clockwise.

⑧ Your paper should look like this. Fold the right-hand point to the left, as shown.

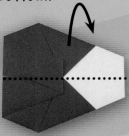

⑨ Then fold the left-hand point to the right, like this.

⑩ Turn your paper over from top to bottom.

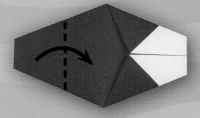

⑪ Fold the left edge to the right, as shown.

⑫ Then mountain fold the paper in half from top to bottom.

Did You Know?

The chicken is the descendant of the red junglefowl, which lives in the forests of Asia.

(13) Make a diagonal valley fold, as shown.

(14) Now fold it the other way so it's also a mountain fold.

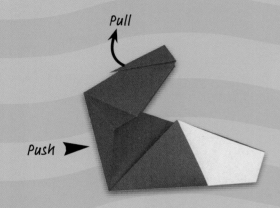

Pull

Push ▶

(15) Push the folds you made in steps 13 and 14 to the left and up to make the neck. Then pull the head up and crease the beak in position.

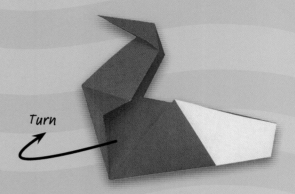

Turn

(16) Your chicken is almost ready to get pecking. Turn it around, so the head is facing away from you.

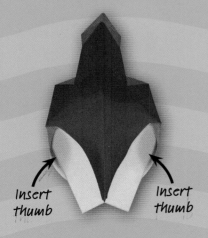

Insert thumb

Insert thumb

(17) Insert your thumbs into the two wing pockets, as shown.

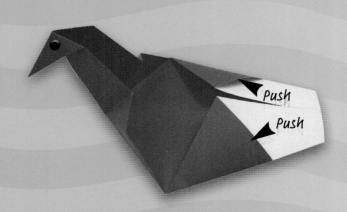

Push

Push

(18) Push your thumbs to the side and the chicken will lower its head to peck. Put your thumbs back together and it will raise its head again.

Chatting Lips

Move the origami lips backwards and forwards to make them chatter. These lips are blue – so they must be cold – but you can make yours any color you want.

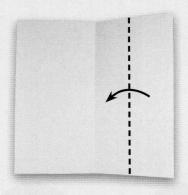

1 Place your paper white side up, with a square edge facing you. Fold it in half from right to left, then unfold.

2 Fold the right-hand edge to the center line.

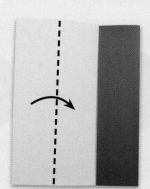

3 Fold the left-hand edge to the center line.

4 Your paper should look like this. Unfold the folds you made in steps 2 and 3.

5 Mountain fold the paper in half from top to bottom.

6 Your paper should look like this. Make a diagonal valley fold in the top right corner, as shown.

Did You Know?

Lips are one of the few parts of the body that can't sweat. That's why they can chap easily.

7 Make a diagonal valley fold in the top left corner.

8 Make another diagonal valley fold in the top right corner, on the fold you made in step 6.

9 Now make a diagonal valley fold in the top left corner, on the fold you made in step 7.

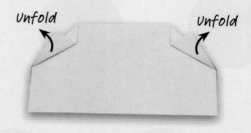

10 Unfold the folds you made in steps 6 to 9.

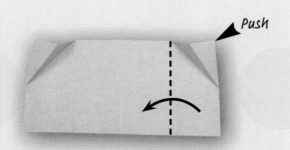

11 Fold the right edge of the top layer to the left. As you do this, push the top right corner down and to the left.

12 Your paper should look like this. Fold the paper back again, but not all the way, so that the top right corner is sticking up.

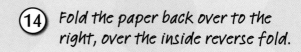
Push

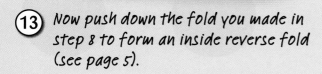

13 Now push down the fold you made in step 8 to form an inside reverse fold (see page 5).

14 Fold the paper back over to the right, over the inside reverse fold.

15 Your paper should look like this. Repeat steps 11 to 14 on the left-hand side.

16 Then unfold your paper, bringing the underside up to the top.

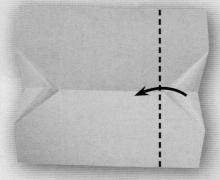

17 Fold the right edge over to the center line.

18 Now fold the left edge over to the center line.

90°

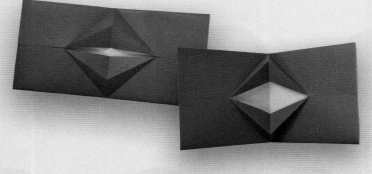

19 Your paper should look like this. Rotate it 90° clockwise.

20 Your lips are ready to chatter! Simply hold the paper at either end, and bring your hands towards you to open the lips. Then push them away from you to close them.

Hungry Crow

Medium

This hungry crow has a great big mouth for gobbling up lots of food. Make sure you have a pen handy to draw in the eyes.

Did You Know?

Crows are some of the most intelligent birds, capable of solving complex puzzles. A group of crows is called a "murder."

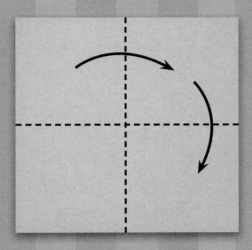

1 Place the paper colored side down, with a straight edge facing you. Fold it from top to bottom, and unfold. Then fold it from left to right, and unfold.

2 Valley fold the top left corner over to the center.

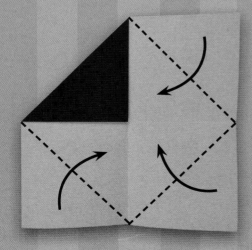

3 Repeat step 2 with the other three corners.

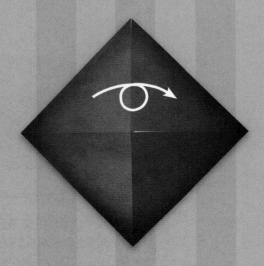

4 Your paper should look like this. Turn it over from left to right.

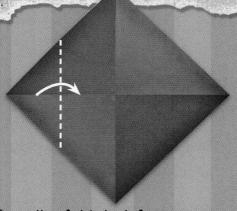

⑤ Valley fold the left corner to the center.

⑥ Then repeat step 5 with the other three corners.

⑦ Your paper should look like this. Mountain fold it in half from top to bottom.

⑧ Start to valley fold the paper in half from right to left, but don't fold it all the way.

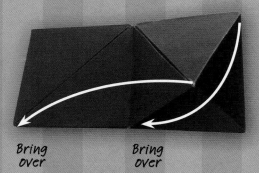

Bring over   Bring over

⑨ As you fold, open up the right-hand side. Bring the bottom right point over to the left, while pushing the top right point down towards the center.

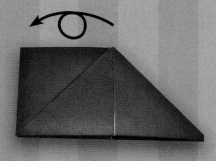

⑩ Your paper should look like this. Turn it over from right to left.

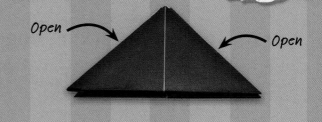

11 Repeat step 9. Open up the right side and bring the bottom right point over to the left, and the top right point down to the center.

12 Your paper should look like this. Open out the folds on the left and right sides to form a star shape.

13 Your paper should be able to stand up on its four points like this. Turn it over from top to bottom.

14 Open up the top flap. This will be the top part of the beak.

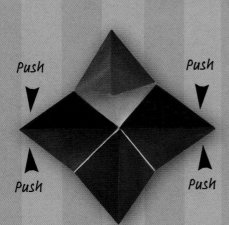

15 Press the flaps on the left and right sides together to make the wings. Leave the bottom flaps open to form the lower part of the beak.

16 Add some eyes and your crow is ready. To open and close his beak, push his wings in and out.

Barking Dog

Woof, woof! This barking dog is very cute. Once you've mastered the folds, why not make him a few friends to play with?

1 Place your paper colored side up, with a corner facing you. Valley fold in half from top to bottom.

2 Diagonally fold the bottom corner of the top layer up to the top edge.

3 Turn the paper over from left to right.

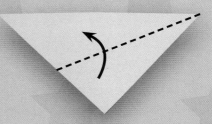

4 Again, diagonally fold the bottom corner of the top layer up to the top edge, so it matches the other side.

5 Valley fold the left corner of the top layer down to the bottom, as shown.

6 Turn it over from left to right and repeat step 5 on the other side.

7 Your paper should look like this. Again, turn it over from left to right.

8 Using the fold you made in step 5 as a guide, fold the left-hand point down to the bottom, as shown.

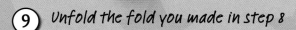

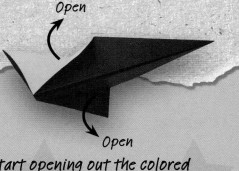

(9) Unfold the fold you made in step 8

(10) Start opening out the colored side of the paper, and turn it towards you.

Open

Open

Push

90°

Unfold

(11) Your paper should look like this. Push the left point to the right to form an inside reverse fold (see page 5).

(12) Unfold the two small triangular folds, front and back. Rotate the paper 90° counterclockwise, then turn over from left to right.

(13) Make a valley fold in the left point, as shown.

(14) Fold it back the other way so it's also a mountain fold.

(15) Open up the left-hand point and start folding it the other way, as a mountain fold. Bring the sides down to create an outside reverse fold (page 5).

Did You Know?

The border collie is believed to be the smartest breed of dog. A collie can understand more than 200 different words.

(16) Your paper should look like this. Flatten it down.

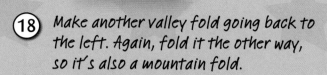

17 Start making the head by valley folding the left point back to the right, as shown. Fold it the other way so it's also a mountain fold.

18 Make another valley fold going back to the left. Again, fold it the other way, so it's also a mountain fold.

19 Now turn the folds you made in steps 17 and 18 into two inside reverse folds (page 5), one inside the other.

20 Your paper should look like this. Make another small fold near the left-hand point and turn it into an outside reverse fold (page 5). This is the nose.

21 Make the tail by folding the right point back to the left, as shown. Fold it the other way so it's also a mountain fold.

22 Make another valley fold, slightly further to the right, as shown. Again, fold it the other way so it's also a mountain fold.

Pull

Hold

23 Now turn the folds you made in steps 21 and 22 into two inside reverse folds (page 5), one inside the other.

24 Your dog is ready! To make him bark, simply hold his front feet and pull his tail. His head will nod up and down (you'll have to add the sound effects).

Kissing Frog

In most fairy tales, the combination of a frog and a kiss usually results in a handsome prince appearing. Here, it'll just provide plenty of origami fun.

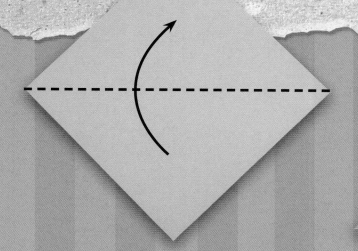

1. Place the paper white side up, with one of the corners facing you. Valley fold the bottom corner up to the top.

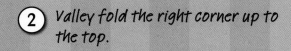

2. Valley fold the right corner up to the top.

3. Valley fold the left corner up to the top.

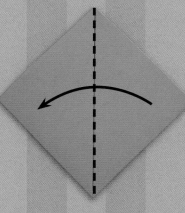

4. Valley fold the paper in half from left to right.

5. Unfold the paper again.

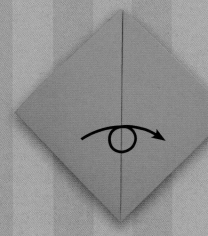

6. Turn the paper over from left to right.

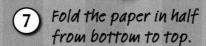

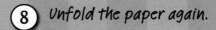

(7) Fold the paper in half from bottom to top.

(8) Unfold the paper again.

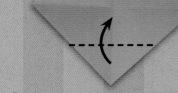

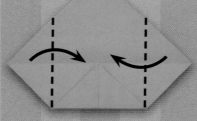

(9) Fold the bottom point up to the center line.

(10) Now repeat step 9 on the left and right sides.

(11) Fold the top right point down to the center.

(12) Your paper should look like this. Unfold the last fold.

(13) Repeat step 11 on the other side.

(14) Unfold the last fold.

Did You Know?

Not all frogs are green, like this one. There are more than 4,000 species and they come in all sorts of colors. Some have bright yellow, blue or red skins to warn predators that they carry a deadly poison.

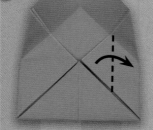

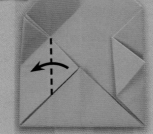

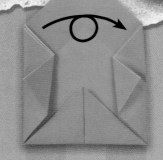

15 Fold the right center point to the right-hand side.

16 Then fold the left center point to the left-hand side.

17 Your paper should look like this. Turn it over from left to right.

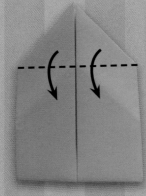

18 On the top layer, fold down the top two points.

19 Fold the center right point up to the right-hand edge.

20 Take the same point and fold it back to the center line.

21 Take the same point again and fold it down to the bottom point of the triangle.

22 Open up the two pieces of paper in the fold you made in step 21.

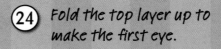

Push

23 Your paper should look like this. Press it down.

24 Fold the top layer up to make the first eye.

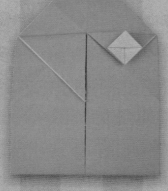

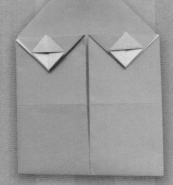

25 Now repeat steps 19 to 24 on the left-hand side to make the second eye.

26 Your paper should look like this. Turn it over from left to right.

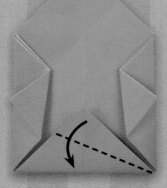

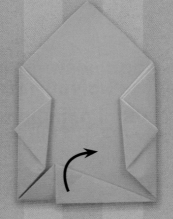

27 Make a diagonal valley fold in the bottom triangle starting from the right-hand corner, as shown.

28 Unfold the fold you made in step 27 and then make the same fold on the left-hand side.

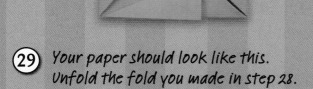

29 Your paper should look like this. Unfold the fold you made in step 28.

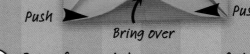

Push   Bring over   Push

30 Bring forward the top point of the bottom triangle and push the folds you made in steps 28 and 29 towards each other to form the feet.

31 To make the mouth, fold down the top point of the top layer, but don't crease. Curve it slightly so it's pointing upwards. This is the bottom half of the mouth.

32 Bring the top of the mouth down and curve it slightly so it's pointing downwards.

33 To get your frog prince to pucker up, simply press his sides together.

 Press

 Press

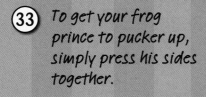

Glossary

chatter Either to talk quickly without stopping, or to make clicking sounds by knocking something (such as teeth) together again and again.

crease A line in a piece of paper made by folding.

descendant An animal or plant that is related to a particular animal or plant that lived a long time before them.

gulp To swallow something quickly and often noisily in a large mouthful.

handsome To be very good-looking.

mountain fold An origami step where a piece of paper is folded so that the crease is pointing upwards, like a mountain.

predator An animal that eats other animals.

step fold A mountain fold and valley fold next to each other.

streamlined Designed to move as quickly as possible through air or water.

valley fold An origami step where a piece of paper is folded so that the crease is pointing downwards, like a valley.

Further Reading

Akass, Susan. *My First Origami Book*. Cico Kidz, 2011.
Ono, Mari. *Origami for Children*. Cico, 2009.
Robinson, Nick. *The Awesome Origami Pack*. Barron's Educational Series, Inc., 2014.

Index

J 745.54 FUL

Fullman, Joe.

Snapping and speaking origami

APR 1 9 2016